Dr. Aruna Polisetty, Jikku Susan Kurian & Vijaya Kittu Manda

BASICS OF TRADE AND COMMERCE

-An introductory guide to business essentials

Authors

DR. ARUNA POLISETTY, JIKKU SUSAN KURIAN & VIJAYA KITTU MANDA.

Business is seen as a risk. Anyone who thinks of taking it up is often discouraged by his family, friends, and others because of stereotyped meaning and thinking attached to entrepreneurship.

Only those free in spirit and love to perform in ever-changing circumstances with enthusiasm are eligible to do it.

The moment someone starts a business with a doubtful mind

of either making or losing money, things are sure to gravitate towards the reality which is fed more. So, negating any negativity created around the business is the first step one must practice.

Business, big or small, is GREAT!! Only those communities and families who *appreciate, practice, and see it as good are rich, affluent, and fortunate!!*

It is indeed opening you up to the world of opportunities through

A holistic profession.

This book will help all who incessantly strive to come out of their comfort zones and achieve financial freedom through business. This manual is full of a glimpse of the important elements of the business.

Deliberate efforts have been made to be very precise with information so that one imbibes and remembers its relevance and importance. Any business is all about possibilities, responsibilities, and intuition. There are so many things that cannot be taught. You will develop more and more clarity and learn through your experiences on the way, as all the pieces of the puzzle will fall into place only once you set off for it.

A good deal of information leads to decisions and actions that strengthen the prospects of a startup. Nevertheless, it's always a sensible thing to avoid common mistakes, more likely expensive Beginner's mistakes!!

We wish you all a very Happy BUSINESS!!

Fundamental Concept

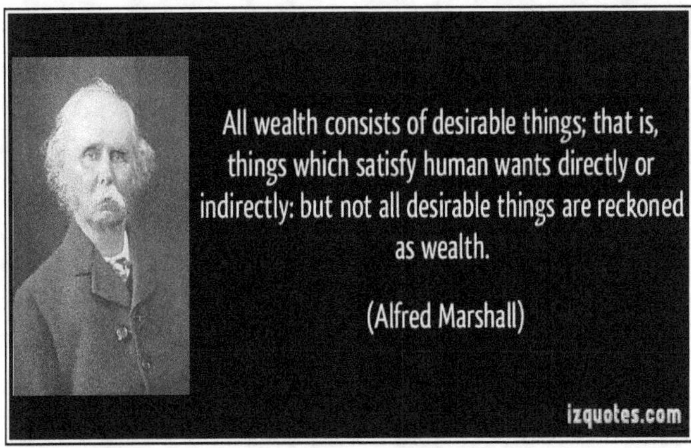

Every human being executes many activities in his daily life. He always keeps himself fit in some or other kind of activities to satisfy his Physiological Needs (survival needs such as Air, food, cloth, shelter reproduction, etc.) and social needs (sense of Belongingness, intimacy, responsibility towards friends, relationships, society, etc.)

Hence, the activities done by human beings are to satisfy his survival needs (generation of wealth) or personal interest (personal commitment /social obligation). Irrespective whether to meet physiological needs or social needs, his activities divided into

1. Economic Activities
2. Non-economic Activities

ECONOMIC ACTIVITIES

The activities carried out in wealth generation to lead life are known as economic activities. The main objective of such events is to earn money for meeting personal obligations such as food, clothing, shelter, etc. An individual who is the officer in a factory, an industrialist, produces goods. The following are examples of economic activities. The lawyer is a legal assistant to a person who renders his services for money. A doctor who treats his patients for fees. A farmer interested in crops and livestock and earn returns on his investment made on plants and investments.

Similarly, a coolie who works daily for a wage, and a teacher who teaches the students for salary. A sales associate who sells the goods, a businessman who produces products and services, etc. are examples of economic activities.

Hence, Economic activities divided into

1. Profession (Lawyer, Teacher, Doctor)

Nature of work: A specialized knowledge required in a particular area (will be received in return in the form of Honorarium, Fees)

1. Employment (Officer, Salesman, coolie)

Nature of work: Assigned work to be done (will be received in return in the form of salary/wage)

1. Business (Industrialist, Businessman)

Nature of work: Employer (who offers jobs for others for generating profits)

NON ECONOMIC ACTIVITIES

Activities that carry out in satisfying the social obligations, cultural thrust, religious ethics, and brought up values referred to as Non-Economic Activities. These do not aim at wealth generation or monetary benefits. Human beings engage in non-economic activities for personal and emotional reasons. Such as a mother cooks delicious food for her family.

An individual donates blood who are in health issue.

A person donates charity, services at the temple, a group help victims in accidents or natural disasters, etc.

All the above said activities aimed at personal satisfaction by performing.

1. A mother cooks food for the family is out of – Love, warmth, and affection

2. A person donates blood is out of - personal/emotional satisfaction

3. A person gives for charity, services at the temple are out of – cultural thrust, religious ethics

4. A person helps victims in accidents/natural disasters – Brought up values/ social obligation.

Thus, the main objective of economic activities aims to earn money, whereas non-economic activities aim at personal satisfaction. At times, the same event may be economical and non-economic. Let's see how it can be:

1. A nurse attends a patient in a hospital is a commercial activity, and visits to her sick father is a non-economic activity

2. A chef cooks at the restaurant is an economic activity and cooks at home is a non-economic activity

3. A teacher teaching at a school is an economic activity and for her children at home is a non-economic activity

Thus, the same individual may become economical at one place and non-economic at another. The main objective of their work is matters in both.

CONCEPTS OF BUSINESS

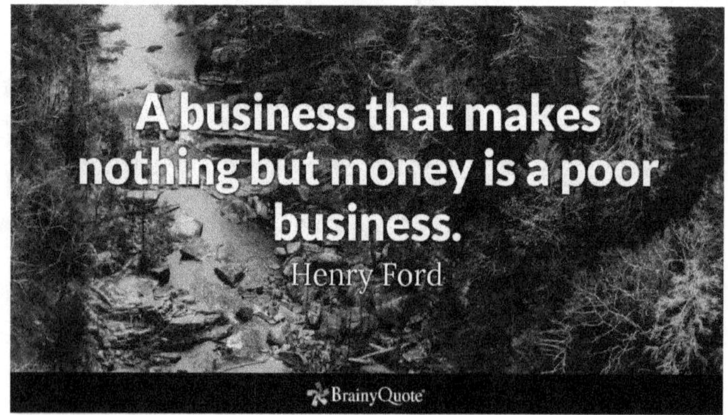

What is Business?

The business represents busyness, being busy – it is an activity in which one keeps him busy. But the economic terms of trade refer to the combination of several works. Combined with time, energy, and efforts to procure, produce, and distribute goods and services to earn profits.

DEFINITIONS OF BUSINESS

According to Urwick and Hunt, "*Business is any enterprise which makes, distributes or provides any service which other members of the community need and are willing to pay for it.*"

Let's see the Characteristics or Nature of Business. Thus, we may easily understand Business:
Human activities always fall between endless wants and scarce resources. For satisfying his infinite desires, he works harder and harder to make use of

limited resources. For generating wealth to satisfy his wants, he makes the best use of available scarce resources (time, natural resources, etc.). It can be a profession, employment, or business.

CHARACTERISTICS OR NATURE OF BUSINESS

The nature of business /characteristics of business is classified based on the kind of activities.

Based on Main Activities

1. It deals with the Procurement of inputs such as Capital, Labor, Materials, Machinery, Technology, etc.; thus, it generates employment
2. It deals with the production, either tangible goods or intangible service, by combining all the inputs with efforts, proper planning, and execution.
3. It deals with the sale of output in the targeted market by creating awareness, reaching the masses,

positioning your name. Thus, it leads to the growth of the economy by its profit generation.

Based on Auxiliary Activities

1. Transportation of products to various places, it may be raw materials or finished products. Bringing the products from the supplier place to the manufacturer's place or sending them from the manufacturer's place to outlets.
2. Warehouse the goods which are not sold (finished products) or not been used (raw materials)
3. Ensure the business assets such as machinery, buildings, commodities, etc. are insured. Hence there is a threat in terms of risk and uncertainty.
4. Banking services to facilitate money requirements in terms of loans, overdraft facilities, etc.

Thus, business is defined as a continuous process, deals only with commercial activities that involve money. It can be any activity, procurement, production, sale or transporta tion, warehousing, insurance, or banking concerned in creating wealth by assuming risk and uncertainty during the generation of revenue /profit.

Thus, it satisfies his desires and societal benefit; hence, it generates employment and leads to its growth.

Characteristics of Business

1. The business establishes on up-gradation of an existing proposal, innovative initiative, or an invention.

2. Business operations are continues process, uses resources optimally

3. Business generates Employment

4. It deals with Goods or services

5. Deals only with monetary activities

6. It assumes risk and uncertainty

7. The firm aims at satisfying the customer needs

8. The business provides information to the stakeholders / interested parties

9. It obliges government interference, finally

10. It aims at generating Profits

In general, the main objective is to make a profit. But in practice, it cannot be the only objective of the business. While attaining the aim of making a profit, business firms keep the interest of their owners in view. However, a business firm cannot ignore its consumers, employees, the community, and society. For instance, no business can flourish in the long run until and unless fair wages are paid to the employees and reach the consumers' expectations. A business firm enjoys a steady place in the market and well-positioned in the minds of the consumers only if it follows specific aspirations. Business objectives have to aim not only at profit generation but also the well-being of employees, consumers, society as a whole.

Thus, the objectives of business classified as

a. Economic Objectives

b. Social Objectives

c. Human Objectives

d. National Objectives

e. Global Objectives

Let us look into these objectives in detail.

ECONOMIC OBJECTIVES

The economic objectives of business refer to the aim of earning profit. To arrive at this objective, along with profit motive firm has to aim at optimum utilization of resources, establishing new consumers, continues innovations in the product range.

Let us learn about these in detail.

a) Profit Motive

Profit is the means of business, without which no company can carry on in a competitive market. Profit-making is the primary objective for which a business unit is expected and brought into existence. Profits have to be earned to grantee the survival of the business, its growth, and its expansion, besides, by reinvesting a part of earnings in extending the market to grab new consumers and upgrading the product, diversification into different products lines over a while to achieve the prime objective.

b) Creation of customers

No market is a monopoly; the availability of substitutes is enormous due to severe competition. The primary task in the hands of businessmen is not only to retain their customers but also to ensure that new customers will create. This scenario is possible only when he produces qualitative and safe products.

c) Continues innovations

The aggressive competition in the markets leads to regular innovations. The innovations can be in the form of product innovation, process innovation, promotion, and innovation. Business people need to ensure it reaches the masses on time by adopting better methods, attracting new promotional techniques. Better practices and modern procedures and reducing selling price through the effective use of resources leads to generating profits continuously.

d) Best possible use of resources

As markets are price-sensitive, offering the products at lower prices is a strategy to grab the market. However, it does not promise all the time to provide products at lower prices. To get the benefits out of pricing strategies, firms have to ensure the usage of resources at optimum to get the product at a lower cost. The employment of efficient workers, making full use of machines and minimizing the waste of raw materials, etc. may lead to reach the objectives of the firm.

SOCIAL OBJECTIVES

Social objectives of business refer to the aim of being responsible towards society; a firm's activities are socio-economic. To arrive at this objective, firms have to concentrate on the production and distribution of qualitative goods and services. It shall not create any trouble to the society, and generous towards respective local and state authorities in practicing fair trade practices and thus leads to the general welfare of the community.

Let us learn about these in detail.

i. **Manufacture and supply of qualitative goods/products and services.**

While the business utilizes several resources of the society, the public anticipates getting quality goods and services from the business units. The business objective should be to produce superior quality goods and deliver them to the right place and the right time. It is not expected from the businessman to supply infected or inferior products that cause harm to the customers. Business units should charge the price according to the quality of the goods and services provided to society. At the same time, consumers also expect timely supply.

ii. Implementation of fair trade policies and practices.

Activities such as black-marketing, hoarding, and over-charging are considered as adverse in every society. Besides, deceiving advertisements often give a false impression of the quality of products. Such advertisements mislead the customers, and the businessmen use them for the sake of making huge profits. Simultaneously, business units must not create any artificial scarcity of essential goods to raise prices to earn more profits. All these activities receive an awful name and make the businessmen liable for penalty and even imprisonment. Therefore, the business's objective should be to adopt fair trade practices for the welfare of consumers and society.

iii. Corporate Social Responsibility

It is expected from every business unit to work for the general welfare and support society. Social responsibility activities include supporting schools and colleges for better education and opening vocational training centers to train people to earn their livelihood. To help the needy, establishing hospitals for medical facilities and providing recreational facilities for the general public like parks, sports complexes, etc.

HUMAN OBJECTIVES

Human objectives refer to the goals aimed at the well-being and the execution of expectations of employees and other stakeholders of the business. Thus, the human aspirations of business activities may include the employees' economic welfare, social and psychological satisfaction of employees, and other stakeholders.

i. Financial security of the employees

Financial security is expected by individuals who work with the organization; simultaneously, the employer has to feel accountable for the employees and provided fair remuneration and additional incentives for higher performance. Reimbursement of provident fund, pension, and other facilities like medical services, housing facilities, etc. with this, they feel more satisfied at work and positively contribute more to the business.

ii. The social and emotional satisfaction of employees

It is an obligation to all business units to provide social and emotional satisfaction to their employees. It is possible only when recruiting the right person for the right job. Making the work more exciting and challenging and creating opportunities for promotion and improvement in career. Not only concentrating on motivating but also have to look after their grievances and needs to respond to their problems immediately.

iii. Progress of employees/ human resources of the organization

Employees, as human beings, with a general human tendency, they always want to grow. To improve the career graph for the employees, employers need to provide them with proper training and development activities. Hence, their skills, talents, and competencies will enhance.

iv. The well-being of stakeholders of the business

Business units need to provide accurate information to their stakeholders such as creditors, investors, government, tax authorities, suppliers, etc., by providing factual financial statements on time.

NATIONAL OBJECTIVES

National objectives aim to derive from national goals and interests. Resources of the nation are applied in direct relation with the goals and interests of the government.

i.   Generation of employment

One of the business's prime national objectives is to create opportunities for talented people in the nation. The generation of employment can be attained by establishing new business units, expanding markets, amplify distribution channels, etc. At the same time, business people need to provide equal opportunity to every person.

ii.   Production according to the national priority

Business units should concentrate more on the manufacture and supply of essential goods and services according to the preferences laid down in the government's plans and policies.

iii. Contribute to the national growth

Manufacturing of goods and services leads to a calculated increase in GDP. Also, the business person needs to report an accurate financial position to the government. It helps in levying exact taxes. Business owners required to should pay their taxes and dues regularly. Honestly, this will increase the government's revenue and thus lead to the nation's development.

GLOBAL OBJECTIVES

Earlier, India had a minimal business relationship with other nations. There was a firm policy for the import and export of goods and services. After the

LPG policy in the year 1991, Export-import policy restrictions have been largely eliminated, and duties on imported products have been significantly reduced. This change had led to increased competition in the market. Today because of globalization, the whole world has become a single market. Products produced in one country are readily available in other countries very quickly. So, to deal with the competition in the global market, every business has specific objectives in mind, that may be called the global objectives.
Let us learn about them.

i. Raise the general standard of living

Growth of business activities across national borders creates quality goods at reasonable prices all over the world. Hence products and services will be available at affordable prices.

ii. Lowers discrepancies among nations

Businesses should help reduce disparities among the rich and developing nations of the world by expanding its operation. It can be possible by capital investment in developing and underdeveloped countries; it can encourage industrial and economic growth.

iii. Competitive goods and services accessible globally

The business should produce goods and services to be globally competitive and have a huge demand in foreign markets. The competitiveness will progress the exporting country's image and earn more foreign exchange for the country.

Functions of Business

Business is defined as the organized efforts or activities of individuals or organizations to produce and sell goods or services benefiting society. To achieve the ultimate goal of a business has to fulfill its functions. The functions of a business are classified into three: internal, external, and support, as depicted below.

Business Functions are classified into

1. Internal Functions
2. External Functions
3. Support functions

Internal Functions: Internal functions are the basic activities carried out within the premises of a business that often lay the foundation of the business. Examples of these basic functions include:

- Obtaining necessary funds to plan and execute the business functions effectively.
- Hiring required human resources to ensure uninterrupted day-to-day operations.
- Managing overhead expenses incurred while testing crucial business activities.
- Sourcing required raw materials essential for manufacturing goods.
- Ensuring the smooth conversion of raw material to finished products.

- Planning advertisement campaigns for promoting manufactured products.

External Functions: External functions include various activities carried out outside the premises of the business. In most cases, the purpose of external activities is to ensure the promotion of various products owned by the business. Examples of external functions include:

- Undertaking a thorough market analysis.
- Executing advertisement campaigns to attract potential customers to purchase manufactured products.
- Customized promotional activities to ensure an increase in sales.
- Identifying sales agents exclusively to gather customers' data.
- Leading promotion and sales of products engaging in various promotional activities.

Support Functions: Support functions are customized backend systems that ensure a smooth flow of internal and external functions. Examples of support functions include:

- Maintaining records of all financial transactions performed by the business.
- Maintaining records of recruitment activities performed by the business.
- Rigorously ensuring the quality of goods produced.
- Identifying non-productive activities and outsourcing it to reduce cost.
- Assigning Public Relation (PR) officers to act as the mouthpiece of the organization.
- Supporting the promotional activities performed by the business.

Though the basic functions of business are broadly classified into these three, it alone does not cover the entire business activities as the scale of operation, and the associated requirements vary across businesses. However, these functions are considered as primary and essential functions by the majority of businesses.

Even though these three business functions are discussed separately, in reality, these cannot function independently. These functions and mutually dependent and rely on each other to effectively execute the respective tasks.

Now let us discuss these three basic business functions in detail:

INTERNAL FUNCTIONS

1. Sales & Marketing
2. Accounting & Function
3. HR & Administration
4. Operations Function
5. Management Information System

Sales and Marketing Functions:

Though the terms marketing and sales are used interchangeably, especially while considering the business activities of a mid-size organization, the two concepts are altogether different from each other and have their own identity. Also, the skillsets required for performing these functions are different.

Sales function involves developing and maintaining cordial relationships with the customers, thereby selling what the business has in stock. This process does not normally consider the interests or needs of the customers before designing a product. Aggressive sales are often undertaken by businesses focusing on profit maximization in a short period. Businesses adopt sales function when the customers do not seek out the nature of the products they sell. Examples of unsought out goods include dictionaries, encyclopedias, insurance, etc. The customers may not take the initiative to buy. Still, a push is required from the businesses' side to make them buy.

On the contrary, the marketing function focuses on the perspectives of the customers rather than the interests of the business. As a result of this orientation, businesses focusing on marketing functions are welcomed enthusiastically by the customers. This function helps the organization to design appropriate strategies to identify the changing interests of the customers, design products accordingly, and communicate the availability of the products so that the customers can buy. The effective marketing function is always advantageous to the businesses as it provides them with the opportunity to decide the price and predict profit. An example of a company's adopting marketing strategy is Apple, where the product is designed according to the expectation of the customers, and it is announced so that the customers can buy.

Accounting Function:

The important business resources are money, and accounting is the function that ensures proper maintenance of all financial records. Various financial data maintained include particulars of salary paid to employees, operating expenses of the business, capital expenditures, investments, donations, cash flow, etc. A business has to maintain proper records of all the financial transactions periodically, which may, in the long run, helps the business to determine its financial strength and weaknesses and also the wealth amassed over a period. The data collected is used in two different ways:

a. Managerial accounting involving the internal application of the collected data that helps the businesses in internal planning to safeguard the smooth functioning of the business.

b. Financial accounting helps to determine the value of a business based on the previous data obtained.

Human Resource (HR) and Administration Function:

Another major function of any business is the HR and administration function, where the HR function concentrates on identifying and bringing in the right people for the right job at the right time. The presence of the right people helps the organization move forward to fetch its long term objectives without any hassles.

Administration, in the context, if business indicates proper management of various operational functions. It also has the responsibility to ensure proper utilization of the available resources, without wastage. It is ultimately the responsibility of the administration to ensure smooth functioning of personnel and operational aspects, without intruding into strategic and executive functions.

Operations Function:

The operation function of a business involves all the activities starting from planning and gathering raw materials to manufacture products according to the requirements of the customers. Another dimension of operations involves gathering ideas from various stakeholders and sharing it within the business organization to improve the process and save cost. The benefit of a well-designed operation function is immense and helps the organization improve efficiency without conceding of employees' safety and health, and avoid possible environmental issues.

Management Information System (MIS)

The performance of all the other business functions in a business organization can be enhanced to a greater extent by implementing a proper management information system (MIS). Management Information System is an information system used for effective decision-making, simultaneously for coordinating, controlling, analyzing, and visualizing all the relevant information in an organization. It may also be considered as a tool to support processes, operations, and intelligence and information technology. MIS generates data-driven reports that help businesses make the right decisions at the right time.

EXTERNAL FUNCTIONS

1. Market Study
2. Commercials
3. Sales Promotion Function
4. Sales Agent
5. Distribution Channels

Market Study

The market study is the process of gathering information about our business from the customers and target audience to measure the viability of the product or service offered. The market study exposes the sources these customers and target audience adopt to fetch information about similar products offered by the competitors. It also helps us to understand the trends in the industry, changing requirements of the customers, the actual benefit customers search from our products, and the factors that influence their decisions to buy a product. A certain market study helps the business gain an edge over the competitors, identifying the changes in the mindset of the customers and providing them their actual requirements before the competitors.

Commercials

A commercial is often considered as one of the best tools in promoting a product, brand, or service. The aim of any commercial is to attract the customers, engage them through the process, which leads to sales of the product. Most businesses use commercials as it is often regarded as a guaranteed method of reaching the target audience. Though pricey compared to other sales promotion activities, one of the main advantages of commercials is its ability to reach masses in the shortest possible time and gain benefits in terms of increased sales volume and high brand recognition.

Sales Promotion Function

Sales promotion is a short-lived incentive initiated by the business organization to motivate customers to initiate a trial or purchase of the product. It includes diverse modes of promotion strategies indented to lift the sales of the products temporarily. Examples of sales promotion include coupons, discounts, scratch cards, buy one get one (BOGO), referral bonuses, etc. The objectives of sales promotion include disseminating information about the brand, creating a market for newly introduced products, gain a new market for existing products, gain the confidence of dealers, and maintaining existing customers with the brand. Sales promotions often give a sudden hike in the sales of the product.

Sales Agent

A sales agent is a person or a company acting on behalf of the organization; he/she introduces products and services to the market. A sales agent, in most cases, is a self-employed sales professional who usually works alone for many non-competing businesses. The sales agent is responsible for attaining orders for the principal organization and is paid a commission for it. The work territory of the sales agent is restricted and is limited to work maintaining those territorial limitations.

Distribution Channels

A distribution channel is a path or route selected by the business organization to reach its customers. It usually comprises of a chain of interdependent businesses or intermediaries that help the finished goods or services pass through them till it reaches the final customer. Distribution channels vary in their level of operation from zero levels to various levels. These channels include wholesalers, retailers, distributors, and at the present times, even the internet.

Support Functions:

1. Logistics Function
2. After Sales Service
3. Information and Communication Technology (ICT) Services
4. Research and Development (R&D)

Logistics Function

Logistics is considered an important and unavoidable support function for any business organization. Though "logistics" was considered a military-based term initially, indicating how the military personnel gathered, stored, and relocated equipment and supplies, the term, over time, is used extensively in the business sector, especially by the manufacturing segment to represent the flow of resources. Logistics plays a significant role in linking the suppliers to the manufacturers and the manufacturers to the customers. Logistics at different levels are used to ensure an uninterrupted supply of raw materials to the manufacturers and finished products to the customers. The roles of logistics are diverse and include assembling of various products, storage, packing, shipping, distribution, consignment supervision, delivery, and information processing.

After Sales Service

After-sales service refers to all the activities the business organization performs to care its valued customers about they purchase the product. In this world of growing competition, the importance of after-sales service is increasing, as the slightest feel of dissatisfaction may result in the customers shifting to its competitor's products. Moreover, present-day customers emphasize the quality of after-sales service than any other factor, as poor quality service becomes chaotic for them to handle. Good quality after-sales service also helps in improving the customer's loyalty towards the company's products, transforming them as the brand ambassadors and reviewers of the product, whom the customers consider as trusted voices.

Information and Communication Technology (ICT) Services

We live in a world of information overload, and this information is perceived in various forms as facts, statistics, intellect, and awareness. ICT refers to every form of telecommunication, internet, computing devices, mobile phones, and the social media platforms used to generate, process, stock, transfer, exhibit, distribute or exchange information by electronic means. In this technology-driven world, ICT provides the base for developing knowledge, initiating innovations, and transmitting information across various stakeholders to a better society. The development of ICT enabled businesses to transfer information swiftly, gather feedback precisely, and make improvements according to the changing requirements of the customers. It gives businesses complete access to the changes happening in the market and adopts appropriate strategies for their benefit and that of the society at large.

Research and Development (R&D)

Research and Development is the lead taken by business organizations to acquire new ideas and knowledge. These ideas can be applied in developing new technology, goods, services, or procedures that can be either used to improve their inhouse activities or sell it to organizations that intend to improve. Methodical research and development help the organizations to uphold its competitiveness as it helps them to focus on the changing trends in the market and also on the competition. Business organizations investing in R & D, in reality, invest in technological up-gradation and future competencies that can be converted as innovative products, processes, and services. The inflow of knowledge brought in by R & D activities have a tremendous effect on developing new product lines or enhancing the already existing processes. Though R & D is considered as a tool at the basic level, the potential it has to bring in a competitive advantage for the business organization is enormous.

BUSINESS CATEGORIES

Business is split into two categories, Industry and Commerce, based on the nature of activities it carries, such as main activities and auxiliary activities. Industry deals with main events such as Procurement, production of goods, and services. At the same time, Commerce deals with both primary and auxiliary activities. For example, the sale of products and the rendering of services; thus, Commerce deals with primary and auxiliary activities. In banking, warehousing, transportation, insurance, etc., both events are needed to run the business. Hence, both are closely related, at the same time, inseparable. In the absence of one, the other cannot work and vice versa. Every producer has to find a specific market for the sale of his products. Still, the producer does not directly relate to consumers.

Hence, the essential part of the Industry is Commerce. However, Commerce is concerned with the sale, transfer, or exchange of goods and services. Therefore Commerce needs Industry for the production of products and services. Commerce builds the necessary arrangement for linking producers and ultimate consumers. It consists of activities involved in buying, selling, transporting, banking, warehousing of goods, and insurance for protecting the products. Trade contains the sale, transfer, or exchange of goods. It does not contain other functions of Commerce alike transportation, warehousing, insurance, banking, etc. If there is no trade, the manufacturers would have to find customers for their products. Thus, without trade, there would be little need for Commerce. Similarly, trade without aids to trade is meaningless, and they exist for trade.

To conclude, we can say that Industry, trade, and Commerce are inter-related with each other. The Industry is concerned with the production of goods and services, and Commerce arranges its sales. Still, the actual operation of sales is in the hands of trade. So they cannot work independently. Thus, to carry out any business and reach its objectives, the Company has put all resources together and proper action. Thus, the activities fall in an organized and efficient way. Subsequently, coordinating and controlling of these activities lead to reach the organizational objectives. This arrangement is known as a business system.

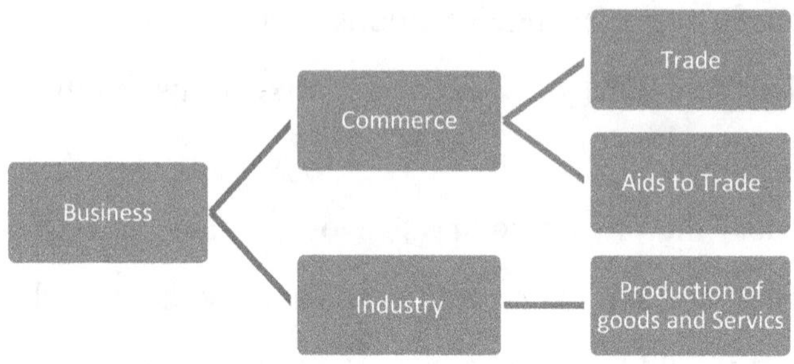

Chart1: Parts of the Business System

Let us clearly understand the concepts of Industry and Commerce. As we realized that, Industry purely deals with production activities, and commerce deals with the sale and distribution of goods and services. Let us discuss Industry:

Industry

The Industry is concerned with manufacturing goods; hence, it deals with converting materials from the raw and final stages. The industry sector may produce producer goods or consumer goods.

Producer goods are made up of machinery, manufacturing plants and materials, and any other product or component used by other firms. Consumer goods are ready for consumption, such as packaged food, readymade garments. Consumer goods are not used in the production of other products, while industrial products are. Consumer goods are tangible in form, can be consumed directly to satisfy a human need or want. Let us see the types of industries based on the type of product produced, investment employed, and type of technology used.

I. Classification of Industries based on the type of product produced is classified as follows:

(i) Primary Industries- Primary industries are those industries concerned with the extraction, production, and processing of natural resources.

These are divided into a. Extractive Industries b. Genetic industries

- **Extractive industries** are concerned with identifying and extracting natural resources such as mining, agriculture, or forestry to convert into commodities and products for the consumer. The outcomes of these industries are either directly consumed or are used as raw materials for further process ex. Iron ore for the Steel industry. These activities are highly mechanized.

- **Genetic industries** are related to the reproducing and multiplying specific species of animals and plants with the motive of earning profits from their sale. Nurseries, breeding of cattle, fish, prawn hatcheries, poultry farms are all covered under the genetic Industry. Even the plants, birds, animals are grown and then sold on profit. Of course, nature, climate, and environment play an essential role in these industries with social skills and talents. Many useful products further use products of these industries by the manufacturing industries. In the case of Extractive Industries, due to extraction, natural resources deplete. But in Genetic industries, the production will be on a continuous process.

(ii) Secondary Industries – Secondary industries are those industries concerned with transforming materials provided by primary industries. The products produced in the primary Industry will become the raw material for secondary industries. Ex: mining of coal is the primary Industry used to generate power is the secondary Industry.

These are divided into a. Manufacturing Industry b. Construction industry

> **Manufacturing Industries** engaged in the conversion of raw materials into semi-finished or finished goods. This Industry generates form utility in products by making

them appropriate for human use. Manufacturing industries produce most of the goods which are used by consumers. These industries supply machines, tools, and other equipment.

➤ **Construction Industries** are those who engaged in the making of infrastructure for the smooth development of the economy. It deals with the construction, erection, or Fabrication of products. These industries are occupied in the construction of buildings, roads, dams, bridges, and canals. These industries use cement, iron, bricks, and wood, etc. for their construction purpose. Technical and architectural skills play an essential role in the construction industry.

➤ **Tertiary industries are also known as the service industry,** the division of the economy that offers services to the general public. These services include a wide range of businesses such as hospitals, financial institutions, schools, and restaurants. Here individuals who are professionals will work.

II. Classification of Industries based on the size of investment employed is classified as follows:

> **Large Scale Industries** are those industries whose capital requirement is fixed by the government that differentiates between large and small scale industries. At present, enterprises investing more than Rs. Three crores in plant and machinery in manufacturing units and ancillary units are covered in large-scale sectors. Large-scale units are in a position to use the latest production methods and economies on various inputs.

> **Small Scale Industries** have an investment up to Rs. 1 crore in plant and machinery is

small scale units. Because the operations take place small in quantity, the major drawback is poor economies of scale. Thus, it leads to a higher cost of production for a lower quantity.

III. Classification of Industries based on the type of technology employed is classified as follows:

> **Heavy Industries** are industries engaged in machinery, steel, power generation, etc., which are called heavy Industry. These industries need heavy .investments and employ high end and sophisticated technology in their production.

> **Light Industries** are those industries engaged in producing consumer goods etc. arc called light industries. The production technology is simple, and the machinery used is inexpensive.

Examples Industries and their Activities				
		Extractive Industries	Metals, Minerals, and other items from the earth.	Drilling, Mining, Dredging, and Quarrying.
	Primary Industries	Genetic Industries	Nurseries, Forestry, Cattle breeding, Animal Husbandry	Producing - breeding or multiplying of certain species of plants or animals
Product-based classification of industries	**Secondary Industries**	Manufact uring Industries	Chemicals, Textiles, Machines, and Equipment	Processing, Fabrication, or preparation of products from raw materials and commodities
		Constructi on Industries	Residential construction, bridge erection, roadway paving, excavations, demolitions, and large scale painting jobs.	Construction, Alteration, and Repair.
		Tertiary industries	It ties up with Primary and Secondary Industries. doctors, banks, tourism, and hospitality industry	Sales, repair services, banking, insurance, business consultants
Investment based classification of industries		Large Scale Industries	Aerospace, Agriculture Chemicals, iron, steel, jute, Pharmaceutical Industry. Defense industry. Arms industry.	use of machinery, employment of wage labor, and the application of regulatory measures for Manufacturing
		Small Scale Industries	Grain processing, machine tools, plastic components for domestic and industrial purpose	Production and packaging

Based on the type of technology used	Heavy Industries	Oil, mining, shipbuilding, steel, chemicals, machinery Manufacturing	Production with heavy machines
	Light Industries	Consumer Electronics, Home and Office Furnishings, Automotive Assembly, Garment Manufacturing, Printing	Production and packaging with light machines

Source: Compiled by Authors

Commerce

Commerce is related to the activities connected with the flow of goods and services for the advantage of producers and consumers in the home country and foreign countries. It facilitates distribution and exchange. Commerce helps in the smooth conduction of business activities; the entire world has become a single market only because of commercial operations efficiency in the respective countries. It acts as a bridge between the producer and the consumer. Commerce is divided into Trade and Aids to trade (means to trade)

Let us understand what trade and types in it are:

*"**The act or process of buying, selling, or exchanging commodities, at either wholesale or retail, within a country or between countries is known as Commerce."***

The essential parts of Commerce are Trade and Aids to Trade.

Trade includes the sale and transfer of goods and services and further divided into Internal Trade and External Trade.

Let us understand what internal trade is:

INTERNAL TRADE

In general, we all use various products in our daily life, right from a notebook, a pen, toothpaste, garments, vegetables, fruits, newspapers, to radio, television, fans, and furniture, and cosmetics. Where do we buy all these products? The answer will be – from the nearby market. Sometimes, during special occasions like functions at home, a celebration of festivals or marriage, usually, people prefer going to a market that is located at a distance from the residence. Now the question that comes up is, how do all these products reach the market? There are several firms or individuals involved in transporting the product from the supplier place to the ultimate consumers. They play as a linkage between the producers and the consumers.

Now let us understand about the intermediaries; they play a major role within a country and outside of the country. Various options were available to consumers in buying the products for their consumption.

INTERNAL TRADE

As we know, goods produced in a nation may be sold within the country or outside the country. When buying and selling products and services occur within the national boundaries of a country, it is referred to as internal trade. It may occur between buyers and sellers in the same area, community, town, city, or maybe in different states, but definitely within the same country. Hence, internal trade is also called home trade or domestic trade/business.

To understand the concept of internal trade, now let us learn about its features.

Features of Internal Trade

- ➢ The buying and selling activities take place within the geographical limits within the country.
- ➢ Home currency payment for goods and services produced in the nation.
- ➢ Internal trade includes transactions between the producers, consumers, and the middlemen at times.

> It consists of a supply chain or distribution network of mediators and agencies involved in exchanging goods and services.

CLASSIFICATION OF INTERNAL TRADE

Generally, we buy goods for our daily use from the local shopkeepers. These shopkeepers purchase products in bulk and sell them to us as per our requirement. But do you know where these shopkeepers buy those goods? They generally buy goods in large quantities either from the producers or from any other shops that sell goods in bulk. Thus, some shopkeepers buy products in bulk and sell to others in bulk. In contrast, others buy in bulk and sell in small quantities as per the customer's requirement.

Thus, based on the volume of goods traded, we can classify internal trade as:

1. Wholesale trade, and

2. Retail trade.

Let us learn more about the types of Internal Trade.

WHOLESALE TRADE

Wholesale trade refers to buying goods in large quantities from producers or manufacturers directly to sell to other traders or buyers in small amounts. Those who are connected in the purchase of massive quantities are called wholesalers. They act as a bridge between the manufacturers or producers and the small traders. Generally, they are specialized in dealing with a similar type of product ex: cloth merchants, pharmacy, hardware, etc.

Characteristics of wholesale trade

Following are the characteristics of wholesale trade:

1. Wholesaler deals with only a little variety of goods and is having specialized knowledge in that specific area. He is an expert trader in a particular line, e.g., machinery, textiles, medicines, etc.

2. Wholesalers buy goods from the manufacturers and producers in bulk and sell them directly to retailers and sometimes to consumers.

3. Since they buy in bulk, goods are available at fewer prices. Trade discounts are an added advantage.

4. Huge capital is required to invest in the wholesale trade. In wholesale trade, purchases are made in bulk; advances are required to be given to manufacturers.

5. In practice, the wholesale trade will do on a credit basis.

6. Due to bulk purchases, it needs extensive storage amenities to maintain the goods.

7. A wholesaler has a direct relation with the manufacturer but an indirect link with the consumers(through a retailer)

8. Generally, people engaged in the same kind of wholesale business are located in one place for convenience. Ex: Wholesale textile market, grain market, scrap market, paper market, etc.

9. Based on the requirements of retailers or by their interest, the wholesale business unit involves in some other activities such as packaging, grading, advertising, market research, etc.

After having some idea about wholesale trade, let us now know about the retail business.

RETAIL TRADE

Retail trade is a trade deal with buying goods from the manufacturers or wholesalers and selling the same to the ultimate consumers. Unlike wholesale business, retail trade deals in a variety of goods. Those who engaged in retail trade are called retailers. Retailers sell products in small quantities as per the requirement of consumers.

Characteristics of Retail Trade

The following are the characteristics of retail trade:

1. Retail trade involves dealing with a variety of items.
2. Generally, retail business consists of buying on credit from wholesalers and selling for cash to consumers.
3. A retailer buys bulk quantities from wholesalers intending to sell smaller quantities to consumers.

4. Retail trade is generally conducted in or near the main market area.

5. A retailer has indirect relations with the manufacturer (through wholesalers) but directly linked with the consumers.

INTERMEDIARIES IN INTERNAL TRADE

Both wholesalers and retailers act as links between producers and consumers in the flow of products' distribution. They are referred to as middlemen as they come in the middle, i.e., between the producers and the consumers in the supply chain of distribution channels.

Chain of Distribution

The role of intermediaries is crucial in the chain of distribution because they provide useful services to both producers and consumers.

A producer gets several benefits.

1. Ease of sale with the help of wholesale traders

2. Wholesale traders buy in bulk quantities; hence producer will be benefited in arranging much for warehousing and holding the stock.

3. Wholesale traders order for bulk quantities; hence producer can reap the benefits out of using the resources optimally, i.e., economies of scale can be reached.

4. The producer role will confine to production activities; thus, he can concentrate on the quality of goods.

5. He can concentrate more on product developments, research and development, since his efforts are significantly less in transport and marketing facilities for the goods produced.

6. The producer will get information related to the demand, tastes, and preferences,

A Consumer also gets several benefits

1. On-time availability of the product at the right place with ease.
2. A variety of products are available in one place because the retailer deals with several products
3. Regular in touch with retailers, hence credit facility also open to the consumers.
4. Consumers can easily share their views with retailers.

Hence, intermediaries in the chain of distribution play a vital role. These intermediaries help in supplying goods on credit, sharing of consumers' and producers' views/feedback, etc.

Based on	Wholesale trader	Retail trader
No. of goods	Deals with few	Deals with many
Purpose (objective)	A sale is a resale	A sale is for consumpti

		on
Source (means to buy)	From Manufacturer/Producer	From Wholesaler
Capital requirement	Heavy	Small
Quantity purchased	Bulk	Small
Location	The same area along with other wholesale traders who deals with similar goods	Located near residential areas

TYPES OF RETAIL TRADE

I hope you learned about the wholesale trader and retail trader features in the previous section. In general, people buy products from the nearby shops in small quantities. In big cities, we see people purchase products from a large shop where various products are available from several counters. This arrangement is available from the people who have engaged in the retailing business.

We can classify the retailing business based on size, small scale, medium scale, and large scales. Based on forms of ownership, it may be a sole proprietorship, cooperative society, partnership, or Joint Stock Company. However, the most common way of classifying retailing business is based on the place they originated.

On this basis,

Retailing business is classified into

1. Itinerant Retailing

2. Fixed shop Retailing

1. Itinerant Retailing

It is a type of small scale retailing. Retailers move around and sell a mixture of items directly to the consumers. They do not possess a fixed shop where they can sell. Selling vegetables, fruits, distributing newspapers early in the morning, selling peanuts, bangles, toys, etc. in residential areas, buses, and trains.

You can see them on pavements in residential localities. In towns and cities, we come across several types of itinerant retailers. Some traders sell their goods/articles on a specific day at different market places. These market places in villages are called "*Haat*," and in towns or cities, they are called "weekly bazaars." The itinerant retailing also comprises persons selling products from door to door. Usually, this retailing does not carry a specific price and is mostly settled by bargaining. However, in most cases, the items sold are not branded products.

2. Fixed Shop Retailing

Fixed Shop Retailing, Here, the name itself explains, retailers, sell goods and services from a fixed place known as a 'shop.' Unlike itinerant retailing, they do not have to move from place to place to sell products to their customers. These shops are typically located at residential locations, market areas, or commercial localities. These shops usually deal with a limited variety of goods. Based on the size of transaction or volume of their operation, fixed shop retailing can be classified as

(a) Fixed shop retailing - Small scale
(b) Fixed shop retailing - Large scale

Let us discuss these two categories.

FIXED SHOP RETAILING – SMALL SCALE

In Fixed shop retailing, a fixed shop has existed, which we can see in our daily like Kirana shops, grocery shops, etc.; these owners deal with goods and services on a small scale. Their objective is to assist in the needs of nearby residential areas. The owners will benefit from direct interaction with customers, know about their tastes and preferences, etc. based on the nature of the products or services they deal with, fixed shop retailing on a small scale can be categorized into:

General store or Variety store: These stores deal with a variety of goods or services. The sale will be made mostly on a cash basis. As the name suggests, it deals with a mixture of products which are mainly required daily, and we can say it as FMCG (fast-moving consumer goods)

1. For example, toiletry (soaps, shampoos, tissues, etc.), snacks, biscuits, hose, etc.

2. Single line store: Single line of goods sold in this type of store. For instance: Garments (only garments are available at different colors, sizes, brands, etc.).

3. Appolo Pharmacy (medicine with different uses will be available).

4. Toy shops (toys of different brands, different prices are available). Categorizations of goods are wholly based on brand, designs, colors, styles, sizes, etc.

5. Specialty store: as the name suggests, these stores deal with a specific brand or a company. All models and varieties of that Company are made available in these types of stores. Ex: woodland, Bata, Raymond's, W, Aurelia, Titan, Patanjali stores, etc.

6. Second-hand Goods shop: Nowadays, in cities and towns, we come across shops selling second-hand goods or used goods. These shops generally sell used products like books, furniture, clothes, and other household items. Online service providers, such as OLX.

LARGE SCALE FIXED SHOP RETAILING

I hope you understood the small-sized outlets from the above discussion. Similarly, several retail shops sell products large-sized large on a large-scale. They come under the large-scale category of fixed shop retailing. Large-scale retailing trade is the type in which a single type of goods or a variety of products is made available to a massive consumer base. Both in a big shop under a single roof or several shops at the convenience of customers or directly delivered at the customers' place.

> **Large-scale Retail Trade types**

In India, commonly, we can find the following types of Large-scale retailing Business:

❖ Departmental Store

❖ Multiple Shops

❖ Consumer Cooperative Store

❖ Mail - Order Retailing

❖ Franchise

❖ **DEPARTMENTAL STORES:**

These are large-scale retail shops where large mixtures of goods and services available in a single construction or roof. Each store has several departments or segments. In each section, a specific type of product like stationery items, toys, books, electronic goods, cosmetics, undergarments, jewelry, etc. are made available. However, all these departments controlled under one management. The customer is offered all types of products and services under one roof. This type is mainly encouraged by people to do all their shopping in one store. These stores also provide facilities like restaurants, movies, games for children, entertainment, clothing, telephone, toilet, ATM, etc., for the convenience of customers.

Departmental stores also provide the facility like free/paid home delivery of goods. They are generally located at the main commercial centers of the cities and towns. That way, customers from different localities can quickly come to buy products as per their convenience.

Big Bazar, Spenser's, Vishal Megamart, Ebony, Shoppers' stop, etc.

- It helps to save time and effort since most of the products are available under one roof.

- Hence it operates on a large scale; management gets the benefits out of the extent of operations.

- Huge capital is required.

- Hence it occupies huge space, usually located far from residential areas. Therefore, they cannot expect customers daily, like small stores.

- There is no direct contact with customers to the management. Employees act as the bridge between consumers and the organization's management for informing about the tastes and preferences of the customers.

❖ MULTIPLE SHOPS

In the previous topic, we have learned how large numbers of products are available under one building or roof. We will now discuss how a manufacturer offers his products to the customers at various places by opening multiple shops at multiple locations. All these shops are identical in terms of products, prices, brand name, range of products, etc. KFC, Mc Donald's, Raymond's, key hotels, etc. are also known as chain stores. Uniformity is a significant observation in all their shops. These shops are located in the primary marketplace or busy shopping centers.

- It caters the needs of consumers at various places
- Consumers feel secured because these are branded products
- No price changes, bargaining is entertained

❖ **CONSUMER COOPERATIVE STORES**

Consumer Cooperative Store is one more form of large scale retailing trade which is owned and managed by the management of cooperative society. When the consumers of a specific area or group find it difficult to get the items of daily necessities, they generally form a cooperative corporation and run the retailing business. They act like wholesale businesses; the consumer cooperative stores purchase the goods from manufacturers or dealers directly and make them available at a lower price.

❖ MAIL ORDER RETAILING

As the name suggests, this form of retailing uses the mailing system (postal and courier) for communication. Once the customer enquired about the product and interested in buying the same. The product is dispatched and delivered to the address received from the customer. However, payment can be made online or cash on delivery.

❖ FRANCHISE

It is like a chain store, but different. It is wholly owned and managed by others, and these shops are run independently by different people at different places. Though it seems like the same appearance, identical products, name, decoration, etc., these independent individuals buy franchise rights from the owner and run the business. This arrangement is a Franchise.

RECENT TRENDS IN DISTRIBUTION

With the development of information technology (i.e., use of updated technology in computers, telephone, Internet, etc.), there are new developments in types of distribution of goods from producers to consumers. Today consumers can conveniently buy products of their choice by sitting at home or office, anytime or night. Due to this excellent reach of goods and services at the feet of consumers, many distribution channels eliminated the lengthy and expensive chain of intermediaries. Manufacturers are directly approaching consumers, either through their websites using the Internet or through their agents (direct-selling).

> **Direct Marketing**

Under this method, no middlemen take part in the sale. Manufacturers or producers directly approach the consumers and sell them the goods and services without intermediary help, i.e., from wholesalers and retailers. The manufacturers inform prospective customers about their products and their uses through advertisements (in newspapers, television, radio) or catalogs, letters, and brochures. If the customer willing to buy the product, he/she place an order to the manufacturers directly over the telephone through a letter sent by post or e-mail. The product gets delivered to the customer through courier, post. There are benefits out of direct marketing to the producer and consumer; consumers will benefit from time and energy-saving and product availability at lower prices. For the producer, he can earn profits by selling the product without recruiting mediators. Transactions are faster when the producer is face-to-face with the consumer.

➢ Internet Marketing

With the widespread use of technology, such as smartphones, computers, and data marketing, made easy. It became easy to buy and sell products over the Internet through websites maintained by producers. Products can be ordered instantaneously from anywhere in the world, 24/7 from the convenience of one's time. On the website, product features displayed, size, color, price, expected delivery, payment options, etc. We can see on the screen just with the click on the mouse of the computer or smartphone, and sales would be made immediately. Thus, the same will be packed and dispatched directly to the consumer. The physical shopping has impacted due to internet marketing.

➢ Telemarketing

Consumers approached by the producers directly over the phone, explain their products, features, and quality, and convince them to buy their product. These are used in services rather than products. For instance, a journal, book subscriptions, credit cards, loans, plots, etc. for contacting consumers, a representative is appointed. They will be in touch with prospective individuals to convert them as their consumers. During the discussion, the representative can make out the interest levels, likes, and dislikes.

EXPORT TRADE

With the developments in science and technology, the scope of trade has also widened. It has now crossed the physical boundaries of each country. The entire planet has turned into a global village. Buying and selling of goods became very easy within the country and outside the country. When two business firms belong to two different nations, buying and selling goods and services are external trade. Usually, we purchase goods from our needs from other countries and also sell our surplus products abroad without facing many difficulties—

the buying and selling of goods termed as External Trade.

No country is self-sufficient in the world possesses everything that is needed by its people. Hence, all have to depend on one other to meet their requirement of certain items. For example, a country may be rich in iron and steel but poor in aluminum. So it has to meet its obligation of aluminum from countries with surplus production of aluminum. Countries with excess production of certain items find it beneficial to sell them to some other countries and buy items in which they are deficient from others. Some countries attain specialization in producing certain products by adopting advanced technology that would benefit from selling excess production to deficit countries.

In contrast, others find it difficult or expensive to produce it in their own country. They prefer to buy those products from the former. Thus, the uneven distribution of natural resources and specialization attained in certain items gives rise to the exchange of products and services. Such a transaction is "External Trade." It is also known as Foreign Trade or International Trade. External trade occurs when the buying and selling of goods occur through the national boundaries of different countries. External trade is also referred to as foreign trade or international trade.

Based on the sale and purchase of goods and services, external trade classified into three types:

a) Import trade

b) Export trade

c) Entrepot trade

a)Import trade

When the business unit/individual of a country purchases goods from another business unit/individual of another country, it is called Import trade. For example, when India Govt.

purchases petroleum products, Electronic goods, gold, machinery, etc., from other countries, it is termed as import trade.

b)Export trade

When the firm/individual of a country sells goods to another country's firm, it is called export trade. For example, the sale of iron, tea, coffee, steel, coal, etc. by Indian companies to other countries is known as its export trade.

c)Entrepot trade

Entrepot trade is nothing but re-export trade. Here, firms import goods to export the same to other countries. The following example will explain entrepot trade: For instance, if an American company imports rubber from Thailand and exports it to Japan, it is called Entrepot trade for America.

Why is there a need for an American company? Why can't Thailand can directly export to Japan?

A country cannot import/export goods directly to each other in a few circumstances. The possible reasons for having this entrepot trade are as follows:

- . Accessible trade routes not existed between the importing and exporting country.
- When imported goods need further processing or development, this development technology may be lacking in the exporting country. This situation leads to entrepot trade.
- Absence of trade agreement between the countries.

Now it is clear how the trade plays a role in internal business trade and external business trade.

We discussed how the goods reach consumers' place from the manufacturer's location. We considered only products.

Then what about services?

What do you mean by service?

How will it exchange between provider and consumer?

To understand these above questions, let us discuss the meaning of services and trade of services. The exchange of tangible goods in the domestic market or international front is visible trade. Invisible trades, i.e., transfer of services (services received and services rendered) in the local market or global face, is referred to as Invisible trade. It can be attached to the sale/purchase of tangible goods or separate based on the need.

Visible trade is defined as imports and exports of tangible goods. In contrast, a country's invisible business trade represents services from other countries or services rendered to other countries. Invisible business trade includes Shipping and insurance services, services to foreign tourists, warehousing services, services of overseas technicians, interest on loans, etc., are some examples of invisible trade. External Trade is a crucial indicator of the economic condition of a nation. Both importing and exporting countries get benefit from external business trade. Although the exporting country earns more foreign exchange by exporting its surplus, the importing country simultaneously receives the chance to use better products and raise the standard of living of its people.

a) **Encourages specialization**

External trade of goods or services will occur when there is a high demand for the products in the international market. This demand encourages the producer to produce more, which, in turn, benefits the producer with maximum utilization resources and can be built at a lower cost. It promotes specialization. For instance, the demand for Chinese electronic goods worldwide results in China's efficiency in this field develops to a greater extent.

b) **Raise in the standard of living**

On account of export trade, exporting countries earn foreign currency; on the other hand, importing countries get qualitative products due to import trade. A country can consume goods that it does not produce. Thus the import and export trade help in raising the living standards of nations.

c) **Improves competition**

Due to severe competition in the global village and free flow of goods and services, several substitutes are available to the consumers; it increases the competition among domestic and foreign producers. The game compels the firms in producing qualitative products. It leads to technological improvements, product quality, etc.

d) **Generates employment opportunities**

External trade and demand for goods and services in foreign markets stimulate the demand for idle resources and facilitate the growth of agricultural, commercial, and business activities, which generates more employment opportunities for the people.

e) **Price equalization**

External trade leads to the equalization of prices of commodities in the world. When commodities tend to rise because of the dumpy supply, it can be checked by importing more goods.

Correspondingly, when the prices of products decline because of the availability of an excessive item, the country may export that surplus to others.

f) **Harmonious relations between nations**

Countries come closer due to an increase in trade; it enhances the exchange of information, demand requirements, understanding the cultures, etc. these activities improve harmonious relations between nations.

g) **Economic growth**

External trade is a vital contributor to the economic growth of a country. It depends to a great extent on the level of foreign trade. If a country specializes in any product, it needs to produce the maximum size to meet the worldwide demand. So, by manufacturing and exporting more goods and services, it can accelerate the country's economic growth.

h) **Proper utilization of natural resources for economic growth**

External trade helps in using the country's natural resources optimally. For example, a state may be rich in minerals. Due to a lack of technological development, it cannot extract those minerals from the earth. So it can import modern equipment and machinery from advanced countries and make proper utilization of those natural resources.

DIFFICULTIES FACED IN EXTERNAL TRADE

External trade faces several difficulties due to activities engaged. Such as internal trade, usually, buyers and sellers meet up together, and transactions occur as per their suitability. But in external trade, the situation is different. It takes a lengthy procedure to buy and sell goods and services. Business people generally face several problems in the process of foreign trade. The various difficulties faced by the buyers and sellers who are engaged in external trade are as follows:

(a) **Distance**: obviously, external business involves long distances; hence the trade activities itself deal with other nations. Except for the neighboring countries, it needs to transport goods for long distances. Therefore it is challenging to maintain quick and close trade contact between countries; it could be a significant difficulty of external trade. Of course, technology improved, and the world upgraded with several communication techniques. Still, physical human existence matters a lot.

(b) There is a substantial risk in transportation: In external trade, both exporter and importer need to bear huge risks. Goods and exporter and importer are at a higher risk; the risk in transit of products is more because of long-distance. Goods are transported by sea, in which ships may sink due to storms or collide with submerged rocks. The enemies may also capture the vessel or goods. Indeed, these risks are minimized through marine insurance, but that increases the cost of goods and is an extra burden.

(c) External trade creates difficulties in communication through modern means of communication that have solved this problem to the maximum extent. Still, it is quite insecure for all sorts of information. Once goods are shipped, it is quite challenging to have quick communication, especially in Air and sea.

(d) Restrictions: External trade is subject to diverse limits by way of quotas, customs, tariffs, and exchange regulations, which confine the scope of external business trade.

(e) Lack of personal touch: lack of personal contact is the foremost disadvantage of external trade. **It is evident that, i**n foreign trade, the transactions between importer and exporter takes place through means of communication. There is no straight contact between the buyer and seller. Hence, the risk of dispute and bad debts are always to be assumed.

(f) Study of foreign markets: to export the products, there should be enough demand for the product; for understanding the international markets, one needs to study the cultural aspects, tastes, and preferences—an extensive study of foreign markets required for both importers and exporters to understand success in external trade. The understanding is not easily possible from an individual exporter's or importer's point of view.

(g) Costly Affair: Completing the required formalities for external trade is expensive and time-consuming because of the high cost of insurance for the goods. Hence, the investment made in transportation should be in safe and secure hands. Thus, trading goods externally is a costly affair.

(i) Alteration in rules and regulations: Every country has framed its own rules and regulations for its external trade to protect its states' economic and political interest. These regulations change from time to time. So the traders find it challenging to acquaint themselves with the rules and regulations and procedures followed by different countries.

i) Regular price change: In external trade, the price of the product frequently changes due to change in foreign currency rate, change in import and export duties, etc.

SPUR OF EXTERNAL TRADE

In the earlier section, we discussed some of the problems and difficulties faced by importers and exporters. Do you think that the traders only carry out the business successfully? The answer is obviously NO. In the process of sale and purchase, the traders need support from others in buying and selling. The individual or institutions that provide various kinds of assistance are referred to as facilitators of external trade.

Let us learn about some of the stimulators who facilitate the external trade:

> **Indent Houses/Indent firms:** These firms help importer and exporter in sending and receiving the order of goods along with other instructions. The import of products from a foreign country can be affected in two ways. The import of goods may be placed by a direct party or with the help of a mediator. The import of goods through a mediator is called an *Indent House*. This indent House may be an independent firm

engaged in a foreign country for trade facilities, representatives, or agents of foreign producers or exporters.

- ➤ **Export Houses:** These are organizations that are registered exporter, holding a valid certification for an export house, issued by the Director-General of foreign trade (in India) different for different countries. These export houses are involved in export promotion activities, such as Handloom Export Corporation (HHEC), MMTC, Handicrafts, STC, and Central Cottage Industries Corporation (CCIC), etc.

- ➤ **Forwarding Agents:** A *forwarding agent* is an individual, an *agency*, or a business involved in collecting goods, shipment, and delivery of goods. It organizes transfers for individuals or other companies to act on behalf of exporters to complete all the formalities of loading the products on the ship.

➢ **Clearing Agent:** Clearing agent is an authorized individual or a firm who act on behalf of the importer and fulfill all formalities required for making the goods from the port of destination. He takes delivery of the products from the customs authority and sends the goods by rail/road to the importer's place.

➢ **Shipping Company:** It transports goods on payment of freight charges and delivers the same to the importer.

➢ **Insurance Company:** Insurance Company insures the goods and bears the loss or damage to the insured products against insured risks right from the exporter place to the importer place.

➢ **Trade Commissioners and Representatives:** Trade commissioners are the authorized officials. They are appointed by the government embassy to present the country's trade interests abroad. Trade commissioners collect the information relating to trade relations and discuss the same among traders. They also advise the traders in matters of imports and exports. Representatives guide overseas exporters on behalf of the government of their country. Usually, they make efforts to educate on legal matters and get secure payment for goods.

PROCEDURE FOR EXPORT TRADE

The method generally adopted for exporting goods to a foreign country is as follows:

1. Receipt of inquiry and sending quotations: the process of external trade starts with submitting a query to different exporters by the importer, requesting them to send information about price, quality, terms of payment, etc. In reply to the inquiry, the exporters then send the quotation mentioning details about the products, cost, quality, mode of delivery, terms, and conditions.

2. Receipt of an indent or export order: After the arrival of quotations from exporters to the importer. The importer finds the terms and conditions; when he feels the terms are acceptable, he places an order for the export of goods known as indent. An indent contains a description of the products planned to order, its price, rules, and conditions of delivery, packing, and other information if required. Once the indent is ready, it will be sent to the exporter, on receipt of indent. The exporter forwards his acceptance if he finds it satisfactory.

3. Credit Enquiry: It should be clear to the exporter that there is no default risk in the payment before sending the acceptance to the importer. He should verify the creditworthiness of the importer before the deal. Thus, the exporter may request a letter of credit, bank guarantee.

4. Obtaining an export license: Every country has its import and export policy for free goods and restricted goods. An exporter in India has to complete various formalities and apply for an export license to the appropriate authority. If all the formalities are met, then the export license would be issued. To obtain an export license, the exporter must have (i) an IEC number, (ii) RCMC from an appropriate export promotion council, and (iii) Registration with Export Credit and Guarantee Corporation (ECGC). The registration with ECGC safeguards against the risk of non-payment.

5. Production or Procurement of goods: it is up to the exporter, whether he produces the products or buys them from the market. But he should ensure that the goods must be as per the instructions given in the indent regarding the quality, quantity, price, etc.

6. Pre-shipment Inspection: the Government of India has made a compulsory pre-shipment inspection of goods by certain authorized agencies. This initiative ensures that only better quality products would be exported. Likewise, every nation follows its way of checking its quality before shipping.

7. Clearance of Excise: Manufactured products are subject to clear excise duty formalities under the Central Excise Act in India. Consequently, an excise clearance certificate is a must for the goods to be exported. There are several exemptions for products which are produced exclusively for export in India.

8. Packing and marking of the goods: Production and packing of materials should be made as per the requirements. It also should be done firmly, conferring to the instructions agreed in the indent. If loss arises from defective packing, the exporter may have to bear the loss. In case of any grading requirement, it should be done before packing. The packages should be evident appropriately according to directions if any, so that they may be easily recognized.

9. Selection of forwarding agent: Packed goods may be shipped to the port directly by the exporter or through a forwarding agent (discussed in a spur of external trade in the previous topic). A forwarding agent may work on behalf of the exporter and complete all formalities before shipment. The forwarding agent will be paid for this work.

10. Dispatch of goods by rail/road: The exporter has to dispatch the goods by rail/ road to the port town. He will send the R/R (railway/road receipt) and any other instructions to be followed to the forwarding agent. The agent will complete formalities after the delivery of the goods and ship the same to the importer.

FORWARDING AGENT DUTIES & FORMALITIES

(a) **Acquirement of the customs permits:** The agent has to pertain to the customs office to obtain the license for receipt of goods by providing full details of the products and their terminus to receive the custom permits. A custom permit is given without any delay in the case of duty-free goods. Otherwise, it will be essential to complete other formalities.

(b) **Acquiring shipping order:** The forwarding agent has to assure sufficient space in the ship for the stacking of goods. To get this, he has to fulfill the formalities with the shipping company to acquire the shipping order to enable him to lay the products on the ship.

(c) Export duty payment after **completing the shipping bill:** The Agent must fill in three replicas of the shipping bill and present them to the custom-house. Based on the bill, the duty is calculated by the customs authority. The agent must make payment of the duty and get the original (third copy) of the bill from the customs authority.

(d) Dock dues **Payment:** The agent must arrange for shipping the goods to the dock. For sending the products, two copies of accurately finalized 'Dock Challan' are submitted to the authorities, and a copy of each shipping bill and a shipping order. After dock charges are acknowledged, the dock authorities keep one copy of the dock challan and return the adequately signed second copy to the agent.

(e) **Verification afore loading of goods:** As soon as the ship reaches the port, the authorities of the dock would allow for loading the products. As soon as goods are loaded, custom officials verify for dues, which might not be mentioned in the shipping. The shipping order has to be produced before receiving the goods by the captain or his assistant.

(f) **Receipt of Mate:** After the goods loaded, A "Master Receipt" is issued by the captain or mate. This receipt comprises particulars of the number of goods, number of units, condition of packing, etc.

(g) **Bill of loading:** The forwarding agent will get an authenticated document 'Bill of Loading' once he presents the mate's receipt at the office of the shipping company. The forwarding agent must fill three blank forms of bills of loading by providing details concerning the goods, destination, name of the ship, details of date and place of loading, receiver's name, and address. The bill of loading is either mentioned 'freight paid' or 'freight forward.'

This distinction is based on payment made. The former is when the freight is paid in advance. However, the latter is used when freight is paid at the destination of the port.

(h) **Cargo insurance:** As a precaution against marine risks, it is essential to insure the goods or products. Insurance must ensure that it is made as per the instructions. All details should be mentioned by the importer, if any, declared in the indent. If there are no such instructions, the exporter should insure the goods. After all, the insurance policy is dispatched to the importer.

(i) **Assistance to the exporter:** The agent then notifies the shipment related matters to the exporter. The information includes a bill of lading, shipping proposal, insurance policy, a statement of expenses, and remuneration.

j. Preparation of export and consular invoices: Having had received the advice from the forwarding agent, 'foreign invoice' is prepared by the exporter. The invoice includes and mentions the number of goods sent, the due amount from the importer.

However, a consular invoice is used for easy clearance of products at the destined port in the importing country, and it is compulsory in many countries for custom clearances. The importer may request the exporter to arrange the same consular invoice when needed.

k. Securing Payment: There are two substitute methods by which the exporter can receive payment.

(a) **Letter of credit:** The exporter can obtain immediate payment on the receipt of the letter of credit. The importer's bank may issue the letter of credit in favor of the exporter. The exporter has to draw the bill to get the payment from the bank's local branch in the home country. The letter of credit has been issued on behalf of the importer's bank.

(b) **Letter of hypothecation:** When the exporter wants to receive payment instantly, he can obtain the bill (accepted by the importer) discounted in his bank. To do so, the exporter has to give a letter of hypothecation to his bank. A letter of hypothecation is attached to the bill of exchange, which is accepted by the importer. A letter of hypothecation allows the exporter to sell goods. However, in case of dishonor of the bill, the bank realizes the amount from the exporter.

IMPORT TRADE PROCEDURE

The steps involved in the process of importing goods:

a. **Trade inquiry:** It is a written request sends by the importer to the eligible exporters for the supply of appropriate information regarding the terms and conditions, price, quality, the number of goods required to be exported. The exporter prepares quotations and sends it to the importer after the trade inquiry of the importer.

b. **Obtaining import license:** both importer and exporters need to have a proper license to import or export the goods. Hence, an importer imports goods after obtaining a valid license from the Import Licensing Authority (In India, the import license can be obtained) it is compulsory to get the IEC (Importer Exporter Code) number from the DGFT (Directorate General of Foreign Trade).

c. **Obtaining foreign exchange: In India,** foreign exchange transactions are controlled by RBI (Reserve Bank of India); the importer has to apply along with necessary documents to the Exchange Control Department of RBI. After scrutinizing the application, the RBI will endorse the issue of foreign exchange transactions.

d. **Placing the Indent:** Indent is the purchase order by an importer to the exporter for definite goods. Finally, the indent may be sent to the manufacturer directly or the exporting agent.

e. **Sending a letter of credit:** since there is no direct interaction between exporter and importer in external trade, the parties are not very well known to each other. So the exporter wants to know the credibility of the importer. Generally, the exporter requests the importer to dispatch a letter of credit. Thus, an importer can get a letter of credit as per the terms and conditions of his banker, finally sends it to the exporter. It ensures payment of a bill of exchange drawn by the exporter up to the amount indicated in the letter of credit.

f. **Procuring the shipping details:** The importer will arrange to obtain necessary documents such as a bill of lading, shipment bill, etc., later receiving the advice letter from the exporter. An importer is required to make payment in exporter's bank to obtain the essential documents for taking delivery of the goods.

g. **Appointment of clearing agent:** The importer may take delivery on his own or appoint an agent known as a clearing agent, to take delivery of the goods. The importer sends required documents to his agent for the clearance of goods. The clearing agent would be paid commission for his services.

FORMALITIES TO BE CONCLUDED BY THE CLEARING AGENT

a. **Endorsement for delivery:** When the ship reaches the port, the clearing agent approaches the concerned shipping company and gets the bill of lading endorsed in his name from the shipping company. If the exporter has not paid the freight, it will have to be paid before the endorsement of the bill of lading.

b. **Bill of entry:** The agent has to complete the formalities and submit three copies of the bill of entry to the customs authority. The clearing agent has to pay all dues that are estimated by the customs authority.

c. **Payment of dock charges:** The agent is subjected to finish the formalities and file two copies and three copies of the Port Trust receipt and Bill of entry respectively to the landing and shipping dues office. After receiving the dock charger, the dock authority will return one and two copies of the Port Trust receipt and Bill of entry respectively to the agent. Subsequently, the agent has to submit this copy and two copies of the Bill of entry to the customs office. If customs duty is paid in advance, then he will take delivery of the goods.

d. **Dispatch of goods by Rail/Road:** The clearing agent has to layout carriage of the goods to the transport authority or railway station later taking the delivery from the dock authority. He will dispatch the goods by rail/road to his principal and get the railway receipt/carrier receipt.

e. **Advice to the importer:** The agent has to compose a letter of advice to the importer after shipment of goods. In this letter, information about the arrival of goods and their dispatch by rail or road is specified. He has to confine with it, the railway receipt/carrier receipt, and a statement of his expenses and charges.

f. **Delivery of goods from Transport /Railway Authorities:** The importer can proceed for delivery of the goods from the transport or railway authority and carry them to his go down.

AIDS TO TRADE

Aids to trade are auxiliary activities that facilitate the Industry and Trade activities.

Aids to trade are supporting activities that help the main activities, such as Insurance, Banking, Transport, Warehousing, and advertising communication. These are auxiliaries to trade; these support not only trade but also industry. Hence, the entire business activity is complete with the presence of Aids to trade. The auxiliaries to business are discussed below:

Insurance

Insurance: Insurance is a contract, presented by a policy, where an individual or entity receives financial protection or compensation besides losses from an insurance company. The insurance company pools clients' risks to make payments more reasonable for the insured person or property. Insurance policies are used to protect from financial losses, either big or small. Insurance Policy: insurance policies are contracts that provide people with financial security from future uncertainties. Certain important principles must be upheld (discussed in the upcoming topic) to enter into an insurance policy or contract.

Types of insurance

1. Life Insurance
2. General Insurance or Non-life Insurance.

Life Insurance: Life Insurance is an agreement promise for payment of a sum of money to the person assured or, following him to the person entitled to receive the same, on the happening of death of a Peron. It is a good method to protect your family financially, in case of death, by providing funds for the loss of regular income.

General insurance: General Insurance is taken for other than the life of a human. It can be many types of Health insurance, Fire Insurance, Marine Insurance, Accident Insurance, Auto insurance, Cattle Insurance, Travel Insurance, Health Insurance, Disability Insurance, etc.

Because we are discussing business, now let us discuss how the insurance will help in business activities. As we know future is uncertain; even if you have a flourishing business, disaster could strike at any instant and force you to shut your doors. Companies naturally take an insurance policy to mitigate the risk of unforeseen damage. At the same time, it might seem alluring to cut costs by forgoing insurance. However, business experts like Small Business Administration (SBA) suggest maintaining an insurance policy.

Considerations

It is better if you had business insurance to cover loss due to natural disasters and general liability, such as malpractice. For instance, a patient might sue a doctor's practice; instead of that, if the doctor's assistants give him some wrong medication? Similarly, if your business premises are under a flood zone. A flood may collapse your business properties and allow competitors to enter your market while you are in the rebuilding process.

Legal Requirements

States regularly require certain types of business insurance. According to the SBA, if you have employees, you must purchase worker's compensation coverage through the state or a commercial provider.

It is a general tendency in businesses; owners feel that business insurance is an expenditure they cannot afford for it or is a luxury for well-established businesses. It is true; business insurance is expensive; it is an expense for every business, regardless of the nature of the product you deal with, based on size or length of time in existence, which needs to include in its budget. However, insurance protects a business from closing due to a shattering loss. History was proof for closing the businesses due to Fires, floods, tsunami, etc. When a company accepts insurance against losses, closure and loss are considered only temporary but not permanent. It is suggested that every Company should consider business interruption insurance always, a rider on their insurance, to make sure continued cash flow for the duration of a closure due to its advantages:

- Business liability insurance covers the loss incurred on the business premises, accidents at your premises, defects of your products, etc., can be covered if your business is insured. For ex: If a customer slips and falls while on your business premises on business hours or your product has a deficiency, and that injured a customer, and you do not have insurance, this could lead to the closure of your business. If an employee met an accident and got injured would be disastrous as well.

- Thefts may take place in new business premises and is a big target for thieves due to less security initially, not perfect in all the activities. Computers, office furniture, and other equipment are worth more at a pawn or chop shop than older equipment. Similar to that, an older business that has made renovations and renewals are a target. In that case, Replacement insurance protects a business in the incident equipment is stolen, or replacement of the missing items and paying for repairs from damage caused by the invasion.

- The amount of insurance to carry will depend on your industry, the business structure, and the number of assets your business has. Depend on which one needs to insure their risks against any unforeseen losses.

Seven Insurance Principles

1. The principal of **Utmost Good Faith**: The principle of utmost good faith appeals to

both the insured and insurer to provide adequate and transparent information. While they enter into the contract, the insurer must provide complete details of the insurance contract. Similarly, the insured is required to provide details to the insurer with that influence the subject matter.

For example – Kishore took health insurance policy; however, at the time of taking the policy, he was a smoker and drinker, and he didn't disclose this fact. He got cancer. The insurance company won't pay anything because the insured has not entered the contract with faith. He is not fair in revealing the facts.

2. **Principle of Insurable Interest:** Insured should have an insurable interest in the subject matter. In a life insurance policy, the spouse and dependents should have an insurable interest in the life of the insured. Even business corporations should have insurable interests in the life of their employees. In the case of marine insurance

or life insurance, the insured should be the owner both when entering policy. Otherwise, at least,   the insurance contract at the time of the accident.

3. **Principle of Indemnity:** The indemnity principle stresses on coverage of losses. It is subjected to cover losses, not to make profits out of policy. Insured is not entitled to make any profit out of the insurance contract. Of course, this policy does not apply to life policies.

4. **Principle of Contribution:** In the case of an insured person taken more than one insurance policy for the same cause or subject matter, the Insured can not make profits by claiming for the same loss from more than one policy.

For example - Raju has a property worth Rs.50, 00,000. He took insurance policy from Company XYZ worth Rs.30, 00,000, and Company ABC - Rs.10, 00,000. In the accident, he incurred a loss of

Rs.30, 00,000 to the insured property. Raju can claim Rs. Rs.30, 00,000 from XYZ, but after that, he can't make a profit by claiming Company ABC. Now Company XYZ can claim Company ABC for proportional loss claim value.

5. **Principle of Subrogation:** After making the insurance claim, the insurer steps into the shoes of the insured, and he becomes the owner of the subject matter. Insured could not gain anything by selling the spoiled goods in any manner.

For example - Ravi took an insurance policy for his car. In an accident, his car was damaged. However, the insurer paid the full policy value to Ravi's car damage (insured). Because Ram has received the full policy value by the insurance company, he can't sell the scrap. This principle is called **Subrogation.**

6. **Principle of Loss Minimization**

The Loss Minimization principle states that the Insured must take all the necessary steps to minimize the losses that may be accustomed to assets.

For example - Ram took the insurance policy of his house. In a cylinder blast, his house has burnt. Then, it is expected that Ram should have immediately called the nearest fire station so that the loss could be minimized.

7. **Principle of Causa Proxima:** Several reasons may cause the principle "Cause Proxima" nothing but "Nearest Cause." in practice, an accident. When the property is insured for only one cause, in such a case, the nearest cause of the accident is found out. The insurer pays the claim money only if the nearest cause is insured. Both the insured and insurer have to strictly follow the above principles before entering into an Insurance Contract.

BANKING

A bank is an intermediary that is involved in financial activities such as borrowing and lending money. The activities deal with taking customer deposits, and in return, pays an interest to its deposit holders. The deposits from the customers are used to lend to other customers who need in terms of several loans, such as housing loans, car loans, etc. The banks run on leverage between the saving deposits interest rate and borrowed interest rates. The role of banks in the economy plays a vital role by offering several services. It offers loans from business startups, business expansions, and thus, it leads to enable the growth of the economy.

Without banks, trade does not exist; it may be domestic trade or foreign trade. Internal and international finance for internal and external trade would not exist without the support of banks. Banks make possible the reliable transfer of funds and translation of business practices with in the country and between different countries and different customs worldwide. The global nature of banking also makes the distribution of valuable business and financial information of the countries, businesses, capital markets, and customers. Banking provides a worldwide barometer of economic health and business trends.

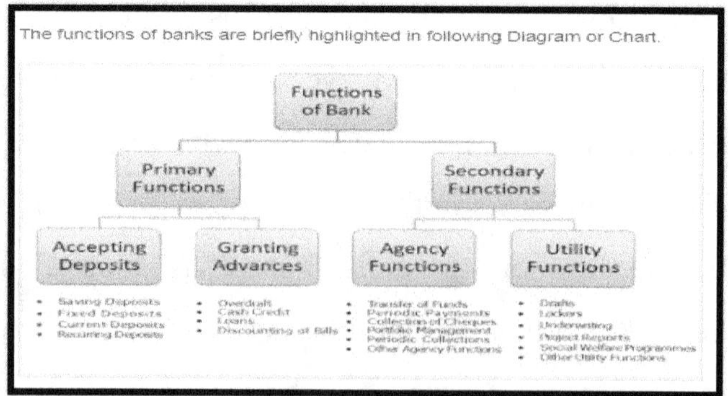

Functions of Banks are classified into:

1. Primary Roles of Banks

The primary role of a bank is referred to as banking functions. These primary roles of banks are explained below.

Accepting Deposits from Savers

The bank collects deposits from the public/savers. These deposits can be classified as different types, such as:-

I. **Saving Deposits**

saving deposits are the type of deposits that encourage saving habits among the general public; saving deposits can be opened in individual or joint names. However, the rate of interest is quite low; even withdrawals of deposits are allowed subject to specific restrictions. Saving account is more suitable for salaried employees and wage earners.

II. **Fixed Deposits**

A fixed deposit is a lump sum amount that is deposited for a specific period. The more the period of deposit, the higher would be the rate of interest is paid. The interest rate varies according to the period of deposit. However, withdrawals are not allowed before the tenure; it is suggested that those who have enough surplus funds should go for these fixed deposits.

III.   Current Deposits

A current account is an account that is carried out by businessmen. But, withdrawals are freely allowed as it is a business account. However, no interest is paid to the account holder; also, there are service charges. But, the account holders can get the benefit of an overdraft facility.

IV.   Recurring Deposits (RD)

Salaried persons and petty traders operate this type of account. Specified money is deposited into the bank periodically. Withdrawals are allowed only after the expiry of a specified period. Usually, banks pay a higher rate of interest for RD.

2. Issuing of Advances and Loans

The bank advances loans to the business community and other members of the public. The rate charged is higher than what it pays on deposits. The difference in the interest rates (lending rate and the deposit rate) is its profit.

The types of bank loans and advances are:-

a. Overdraft

The overdraft facility is given to existing current account holders. For getting this facility, no other separate account is required to be maintained. A certain amount is sanctioned as overdrafts, which can be withdrawn within a certain period, say three months. However, interest is charged on the overdraft amount. An overdraft facility is granted against collateral security. It is sanctioned to people in business and firms.

b. Cash Credits

Every client is permitted a cash credit up to a specific limit, which is fixed in advance. This facility would be given to current account holders and others who do not have an account with the bank. A separate cash credit account is maintained. Interest is charged on the amount withdrawn more than the limit. However, cash credit is given against the security of tangible assets and guarantees. A huge amount is given as advance for a longer period than that of overdraft.

c. Loans

It is normal for the short term, say one year, or medium-term say five years. Nowadays, banks do lend money for the long term. The repayment of money can be made in the form of installments spread over some time or in a lump sum amount. Interest is chargeable on the total amount sanctioned. The rate of interest on loans is comparatively less than the interest rate charged on cash credits and overdrafts. These loans are normally secured against tangible assets of the Company.

d. Discounting of the bill of exchange

The bank can sanction advance money by discounting/ purchasing bills of exchange for domestic and foreign bills. The drawer or the beneficiary will get the amount from the bank after deducting the usual discount charges. At the time of maturity, the bill is presented to the drawee or acceptor. After the bill is presented, the amount is collected by them accordingly.

2. Secondary Roles

Banks not only performs the above mentioned primary functions but also involves in a basket of secondary functions too. These secondary functions, often mentioned as non-banking functions, are briefed below.

1. Agency Functions

One of the major non-banking functions carried out by the banks for the benefit of its customers is agency functions. In this banks act as an agent and various agency functions performed by the bank is as follows:-

a. Fund Transfer

Banks engage in transferring funds from one branch to the other or from one location to another. This fund transfers often eases the demand for the customers to move to various locations to transfer funds.

b. Assortment of Cheques

After verifying the genuineness of the cheque, banks, through clearing, collect funds represented in the cheques for its customer's benefit. Not only through cheque, but banks also collect the money of the bills of exchange.

c. Recurring Payments

Unlike yesteryears, where the customer was responsible for remembering and executing all the recurring payments, banks are now at the service of the customers. Based on the standing instructions of the customer's banks these days assume the responsibility of making recurring payments of the customers. Few examples of recurring payments include EMIs, electricity bills, rent, recurring personal fund transfers, etc.

d. Portfolio Administration

Portfolio administration, often referred to as the process of managing a client's asset spread across stocks, bonds, cash equivalents, and real estate, is also undertaken by banks as a part of its basket of services. Banks, on behalf of the customers, purchase or sell stocks or bonds by debiting or crediting the customer's account accordingly.

e. Recurring Collections

Banks, on behalf of its customers, collect salary, pension, dividend, and various other collections without the customers investing their energy and time to do so.

f. Miscellaneous Agency Functions

Banks of contemporary India act as facilitators, representatives, and managers of its clients, dealing with their assets, liabilities, and numerous financial transactions, representing them at various financial institutions and other banks.

2. Functions of General Utility

The general utility functions of banks also referred to as social development functions, depict the changing face of the banking sector. Under this, the banks will assist the customers with numerous transactions to be completed within a course of time. Examples of general utility functions include payment of telephone bills or other utility bills performed at a center operated by the banks. The general utility functions performed by the banks are detailed below:-

a. Issuing Drafts

Commercial banks issue drafts for transferring money from various locations, thus easing the burden on customers. A draft is a cheque that is drawn on the guaranteed funds of the banks that issue it, making it safer than an individual's cheque while accepting huge payments.

b. Issuing Letters of Credit

Another general utility function performed by the bank is issuing letters of credit. It is a payment mechanism adopted in international trade. A bank issues a document or order to another bank to provide an economic guarantee from a creditworthy bank to an exporter under specified conditions. The letter of credit helps the traders to buy goods on credit as the credit standing of a bank is better trusted than an individual's credit.

c. Locker Facility

The bank provides its customers with a locker facility to safeguard custody of gold, valuable ornaments, property document, etc.

d. Underwriting of Shares

The bank provides underwriting shares and debentures facility through its merchant banking division to its customers.

e. Dealing in Foreign Exchange

The commercial banks are given rights to deal in foreign exchange activities by RBI.

f. Project Reports

The bank may also work on behalf of its customers by undertaking activities such as preparing project reports.

g. Social Welfare Activities

under this, banks will undertake social welfare activities, for instance, public welfare campaigns and adult literacy programs, etc.

h. Additional Utility Functions

this function acts as a referee to the financial standing of customers. Bank collects the creditworthiness information of its clients or customers. It also provides travelers' cheque facility. Market information to its customers.

Transportation

Transportation is in the midst of the important economic activities of a business organization. Transportation helps move the goods from source location to the demanded location; it provides the essential service of connecting a company to its customers and suppliers. Transportation acts as an important tool not only in the logistics function but also in ancillary the financial services of place and time. *Place utility* assumes that customers get the product whenever they demand it. *Time utility* indicates that customers have access to the product when they need/demand it. By working closely with inventory planners, transportation specialists seek to guarantee that the business has product obtainable *when* and *where* customers look for it. Transportation is every so often to blame for a company's incompetence to serve customers properly. Delayed deliveries can be the snitch of service complaints and problems. There is always a possibility of damage incurred while in transit or irresponsibility of warehouse workers, in terms of loading wrong items. Thus, it leads to frustration among the customers, and they may buy from other suppliers in the future.

Yet, when a company performs consistent undamaged delivery services on time can lead to customer confidence for the Company. When a company inculcates faith in its services and performance, it leads to stick to our products and services, irrespective of smart promotions and discounts.

Apart from its service implications, transportation can also exemplify an extensive cost for the business. The transportation cost can sometimes limit whether a customer transaction outcomes in a profit or a loss for the business, reliant on the expense incurred in facilitating transportation for a customer's order. Faster means of transportation normally cost more than slower modes of transportation. Thus shipping an order overseas by airways is much faster than transporting using the ship. Thus, supply chain managers need to examine carefully while considering the cost of transporting goods and have to choose economically.

Logistics is defined as ***"that part of supply chain management that plans, implements, and controls the efficient, effective forward and reverse flow and storage of goods, services, and related information from the point of origin to the point of consumption to meet customers' requirements."***

Transportation denoted, in this expression, concluded the word *flow*. It provides the flow of inventory from points of source in the supply chain to endpoints, or points of utility and consumption. However, businesses administer both inbound and outbound logistics. Inbound logistics involves the purchasing of materials and goods from supplier locations. Outbound logistics implicates the dissemination of materials and goods to customer locations. Hence transportation is essential on the inbound and outbound wings of the business.

The meaning of *logistics* mentions both forward flow and storage of goods, services, and related information, and reverse flow too.

Inventory sometimes flows in the reverse direction. *Reverse logistics* refers to "**the role of logistics in product returns, source reduction, recycling, materials substitution, reuse of materials, waste disposal, refurbishing, repair, and remanufacturing.**" Therefore transportation not only supplies material and products to customers but also transfers reusable and recyclable content to companies that can use it.

MARKETING COMMUNICATION

The existent era of mass communication and cutting-edge mobile technology demands the business organizations to build a novel mix of marketing communication, the purpose being to save the audience from drowning into an ocean of information. The fundamental purpose of this communication mix is to enable the business organizations to withstand the competition and also to remain connected with its target audience. Marketing communication is a strategy adopted by the business organizations, comprising multifaceted measures and techniques through which the information about the products or services offered reaches the target audience. Marketing communication can be defined as the process by which the business organizations attempt to update the customers regarding a product, influence them to purchase it, and at regular intervals, remind them of the products that they sell. Marketing communication is the straight mouth of the business organizations, as it voices the company and its in-house brands to the audience.

Philip Kotler and Kevin Lane Keller define marketing communication as *"how firms attempt to inform, persuade, and remind their customers – directly and indirectly – of products and brands they sell."*

Marketing communication provides a medium for business organizations and their brands to present themselves in front of prospective customers. The rationale behind this communication is to initiate a dialogue with the audience, which may eventually lead to a series of product purchases. In marketing communication, each organization and each product presents to prospective customers, and an exchange of ideas happens between them. Marketing communication can be called a mutually beneficial tool as the business organizations get the opportunity to present themselves to the prospects. The prospects get to know about the numerous additions to the product line of a business organization. Marketing communication is often referred to as a customer-centric activity.

The diagrammatic representation of the marketing communication mix is depicted in Fig.

MARKETING COMMUNICATION

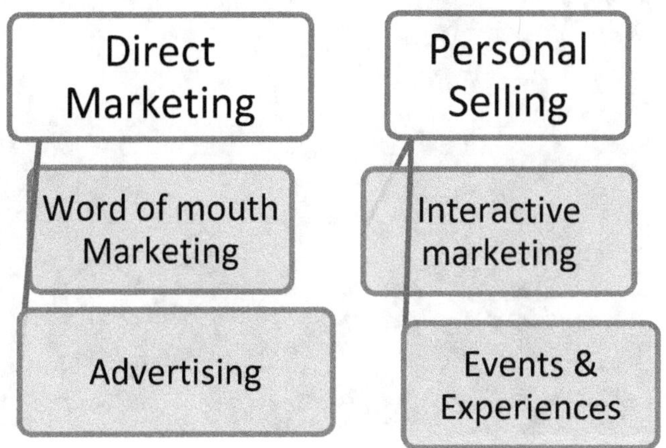

Advertising

Advertising is a non-personal form of communication targeted at the masses to persuade them to purchase their products. Advertising exerts a high level of control to those accountable for designing and delivering promotion messages. Advertisement is considered as the most effective tool by its coverage.

The ability of advertisements to persuade the target audience to the level of purchase is uncertain. Another disadvantage of advertisements is its lack of credibility, as the audience, in most cases, is less likely to believe the messages conveyed.

Direct Marketing

The increased utilization of direct marketing of late by business organizations indicates a paradigm shift from mass to individual communication. In direct marketing, the business organization reaches out to the customers directly using direct mail or tele-calling. Though the customer is contacted directly by the business organization, the absence of face-to-face communication helps the salesperson omit the traditional formalities and concentrate on his core areas to make sales. Unlike mass marketing, direct marketing concentrates on identifying the needs of the customers by individual personal interaction, which may persuade the customers better to try the products or services offered by the business.

Personal Selling

Personal selling can be considered as the most primitive form of marketing communication, which ensures face-to-face interaction between the organization's representative and the customers. In this form of communication, the representative of the business in person discusses the advantages and the disadvantages of the products and tries to influence the prospect to purchase. The benefit of this form of communication is the availability of immediate and, in maximum cases, reliable feedback. The major shortcomings of personal selling is the huge cost involved and less coverage. Compared to advertisements, the degree of control is quite low in personal selling as the salesperson enjoys the freedom to communicate liberally with the customer.

Word-of-Mouth Marketing

Word-of-mouth marketing, as the name implies, is an instance when the customers share the feedback about a product or organization with others. The medium of this communication can be face-to-face or via any medium like telephone, e-mail, social networks, etc. The spread of information through word-of-mouth communication has extensive reach in the age of technological advancements, and any negativity created because of this can have a long-lasting impact on the purchase behavior of the customers. Simultaneously, a satisfied customer acts as a strong campaigner for the product or organization without any financial liability. Business organizations expecting extensive reach can use word-of-mouth marketing strategy to establish their brands in the minds of the customers permanently.

Interactive Marketing

Interactive marketing is not new; it is one to one marketing process still completely different from the traditional marketing methods, where the process reacts and alters according to the activities of individual and prospective customers. The facility to respond to the activities of individual customers makes this marketing technique more viable compared to traditional direct marketing techniques. Interactive marketing is also addressed as event-based or event-driven or trigger-based marketing. Still, the ideology behind all the terminologies remains the same: responding to the actions of the customers and driving up the effectiveness of marketing.

Events and Experiences

Event marketing strategy symbolizes entering a guerilla era where the physical and virtual paths of the customers cross. This marketing strategy provides the marketers with an opportunity to make the customers use the products or services and thereby create a buzz in the market. In event marketing, business organizations can engage in face-to-face interaction with their customers at special events like fairs, concerts, or sporting events. For business organizations dealing with event management, this marketing strategy helps their customers feel and experience the nature and quality of service provided, which is usually beyond any extensive level of communication. Event marketing strategy offers memorable moments to the customers and prospects, persuading them to opt for the product or service.

Public Relations

Public relations is the art of evaluating the trends, forecasting the consequences, and, based on the nature of the organization's leadership, implementing pre-decided plans that will serve both the organization's and the customer's interests. Increased use of public relations and publicity helps the organization build a positive image in the minds of the customers like the level of credibility attached to this form of communication is quite high. Publicity includes disseminating the organization's information through third-party media like newspapers, magazines, or news telecasts; Business organizations also use a wide variety of mechanisms to improve public relations, namely event management, funding, and lobbying. Though it is difficult to control a message that is aired, the authorization offered by the organization's representative adds better credibility to that, and the impact of such messages on the target audience will be far-reaching.

Warehousing

Warehousing allows for timely delivery and optimized distribution, leading to increased labor productivity and superior customer satisfaction. Timely delivery helps reduce errors and damage in the order fulfillment process. Also, it prevents your goods from getting lost or stolen during handling. Warehousing has been around relatively for a long time; it has helped organizations with numerous storage needs. Nowadays, a warehouse no more storage room. Many organizations offer extra executives to streamline your whole inventory network structure.

This makes time effective as the merchandise is possibly cleared when they are required. In this manner, on the off probability that you need to screen and track your raw materials, work in process, and finished goods. A warehouse accompanied by the city can enable them to distribute and mail things to their clients easily. The warehousing facility offers you "security stocking." Preferably, this means your items are accessible for transportation at whatever point clients put in their orders. However, businesses can limit the trouble from flame, robbery, troubles, and harm by using a warehouse to store their products. Also, your merchandise is protected so that you can predict full pay if there should be an incident of any harm or misfortune. Concluding thoughts—warehousing as a business owner, you have different choices, including private, public, and bonded warehouses. Whatever your choice, utilizing warehousing services can streamline your supply chain.

About Authors

DR. ARUNA POLISETTY is an Asst. Professor at GITAM University, Visakhapatnam. A Ph.D. in Finance, she has a unique and simple style of teaching complex business and management topics, which are the spark for several young minds. She guides management students at UG, PG, and Research levels. An avid researcher, her research works are published in reputed journals. Her case studies are published in ICMR

India (Asia's largest case repository) and The Case Study Center (World's largest management case repository). Her research interests include Business Development, Venture Capital Analysis, Human Resource Accounting, Consumer Behavior, and Spiritual Studies. She is also a chair and convener of several national and international conferences. A prolific author, she is the author of several books that are of use for both academics and practitioners. She can be reached at 
arunakovvuru@gmail.com

****

MRS. JIKKU SUSAN KURIAN working as an Assistant Professor at LEAD College of Management, Palakkad, Kerala, has 16 years of experience. Eight years were with leading corporates like Infosys and Omax and the rest seven years with KL University Business School, Vijayawada. A voracious reader turned management professional; she is interested in penning down her thoughts into publications. Hands-on experience in human resources and training helps the author make a good blend of her experiences and management thoughts. She visions the books to be reader-friendly and encouraging, filling enthusiasm in the reader to read. She can be reached at jikkukurian@gmail.com

MR. VIJAYA KITTU MANDA has near to 10+ years' experience in the capital markets. He teaches the concepts of personal finance and financial planning, investing strategies, and investing using Equity Shares and Mutual Funds through his Kittu's Wealth Journey workshops. A weekly columnist, he writes about stock markets and reviews in newspapers. An academic researcher, he authored papers on management and economic topics that were published in international journals. He blogs at GetPaidIndia.com and Asuku.com and can be reached at vijaykittu@hotmail.com

****

REFERENCES

1. http://www.studylecturenotes.com
2. https://www.kullabs.com
3. CSCMP, Thomas J. Goldsby, Deepak Iyengar, Shashank Rao, "The Critical Role of Transportation in Business and the Economy," https://www.informit.com/articles/article.aspx?p =2171313

4. https://kalyan-city.blogspot.com/2012/09/functions-of-business-internal-external.html

5. https://techbullion.com/understanding-key-internal-business-functions-business-organization/

6. https://www.yourarticlelibrary.com/business/business-activities/classification-of-business-activities-with-their-interrelation/69395

7. "An Introduction to 'Business Essentials': Purposes and Plans"

8. Journal of the American College of RadiologyVol. 11Issue 6

9. An Organizational Perspective and a Team Approach: Keys to Successful Business Planning

10. Journal of the American College of RadiologyVol. 13Issue 2

11. The Business Case for Diversity and Inclusion

12. Journal of the American College of RadiologyVol. 17Issue 5

13. What is Interactive Marketing?. https://www.genroe.com/services/what-is-interactive-marketing

14. https://www.accountingverse.com/accounting-basics/types-of-businesses.html

15. https://www.mosourcelink.com/guides/start-a-business/register-your-business/forms-of-business-organization

16. 15. https://yourstory.com/mystory/importance-of-warehousing-to-your-business-ane6qh94o6

17. ANDREA KINNISON, THE SEVEN MOST POPULAR TYPES OF BUSINESSES, HTTPS://WWW.VOLUSION.COM/BLOG/BUSINESS-TYPES/

18. HTTPS://WWW.STARTUPINDIA.GOV.IN/CONTENT/SIH/EN/INTERNATIONAL/GO-TO-MARKET-GUIDE/TYPES-OF-BUSINESSES.HTML

19. https://www.coursehero.com/file/p6n1508t/K%C3%B6lsch-is-only-popular-in-the-region-of-Cologne-so-the-brewery-also-should/

20. INDUSTRIAL SAFETY PRODUCTS FOR PEOPLE WORKING IN HAZARDOUS ENVIRONMENTS

21. The Critical Role of Transportation in Business and the .... https://www.informit.com/articles/article.aspx?p=2171313